SPORTS WHAT'S YOUR POSITION?

FOOTBALL

WHO DOES WHAT?

BY RYAN NAGELHOUT

Gareth Stevens
PUBLISHING

Please visit our website, www.garethstevens.com. For a free color catalog of all our high-quality books, call toll free 1-800-542-2595 or fax 1-877-542-2596.

Cataloging-in-Publication Data

Names: Nagelhout, Ryan.
Title: Football: who does what? / Ryan Nagelhout.
Description: New York : Gareth Stevens Publishing, 2018. | Series: Sports: what's your position? | Includes index.
Identifiers: ISBN 9781538204245 (pbk.) | ISBN 9781538204269 (library bound) | ISBN 9781538204252 (6 pack)
Subjects: LCSH: Football–Juvenile literature.
Classification: LCC GV950.7 N34 2018 | DDC 796.332–dc23

First Edition

Published in 2018 by
Gareth Stevens Publishing
111 East 14th Street, Suite 349
New York, NY 10003

Copyright © 2018 Gareth Stevens Publishing

Designer: Sarah Liddell
Editor: Ryan Nagelhout

Photo credits: Cover, pp. 1, 29 SUSAN LEGGETT/Shuttestock.com; jersey texture used throughout Al Sermeno Photography/Shutterstock.com; chalkboard texture used throughout Maridav/Shutterstock.com; p. 5 Photonimo/Shutterstock.com; p. 6 Air Images/Shutterstock.com; p. 7 Joe Robbins/Contributor/Getty Images Sport/Getty Images; pp. 8, 13, 17, 19, 24, 27 Aspen Photo/Shutterstock.com; p. 9 ANURAK PONGPATIMET/Shutterstock.com; p. 11 Johnathan Daniel/Staff/Getty Images Sport/Getty Images; p. 15 Donald Miralle/Stringer/Getty Images Sport/Getty Images; p. 21 Icon Sportswire/Contributor/Icon Sportswire/Getty Images; p. 23 Scott Cunningham/Stringer/Getty Images Sport/Getty Images; p. 25 Jerry Sharp/Shutterstock.com; p. 28 135pixels/Shutterstock.com.

Printed in the United States of America

CPSIA compliance information: Batch #CS17GS: For further information contact Gareth Stevens, New York, New York at 1-800-542-2595.

CONTENTS

Words in the glossary appear in **bold** type the first time they are used in the text.

PICK A SIDE

Football is a game of offense and defense. The offense tries to score points, and the defense tries to stop the offense. But once you pick a side, both offense and defense have a lot of different positions.

Most people might know what a quarterback does, but do you know the difference between a free safety and a strong safety? And what do they do on running plays? The game of football is constantly changing, and different positions take on different jobs as it does. Let's learn more about the positions that make up a football team!

PLAY SAFE

Learning the different positions in football means learning how to play safely. If you're going to play football, always wear safety **equipment** such as a helmet and pads. Listen to your coaches, who can teach you the right way to tackle, or hit another player. Make sure you, your teammates, and players on the other team stay safe!

FOOTBALL IS A FUN SPORT TO PLAY, BUT YOU HAVE TO BE CAREFUL NOT TO HURT YOURSELF—OR OTHERS!

IN CHARGE

The most important position in football is quarterback. A quarterback's job is to direct a team's offense down the field to score points. They run the offense and are almost always the first person to touch the football. Quarterbacks are very smart. Some quarterbacks call the plays a team runs on offense. They can change plays based on what the other team's defense is doing to suit different situations in the game.

The quarterback throws the football to wide receivers, running backs, and tight ends. Quarterbacks must make plays while avoiding the other team's defense, which wants to tackle them or make them lose the football.

ON THE RUN

Quarterbacks don't always have to throw the ball—they can run, too! Some of today's best quarterbacks can make exciting plays happen with their feet as often as with their arms. A running quarterback can scramble, or get away from the defense even if their protection breaks down in the **pocket**.

HAVING A GOOD QUARTERBACK IS ONE OF THE KEYS TO HAVING A GOOD TEAM. THEY CAN MAKE EVERYONE AROUND THEM PLAY BETTER.

LINE UP

The offensive line is made of the biggest players on the team. Their job is to keep the other team's defense from tackling players on their team with the football. Often they will stay near or behind the line of scrimmage. That's the line on the field where all offensive plays start.

There are five different offensive line positions. The center plays the middle of the offensive line. Centers **snap** the football to a quarterback to start a play. The left and right guards play on each side of the center. The left and right tackles play on the ends of the offensive line.

THE BLIND SIDE

The most important offensive lineman is whoever is protecting the quarterback's blind side. If the quarterback is left-handed, this is the right tackle. If the quarterback is right-handed, that's the left tackle. This tackle keeps the best defensive players from hitting the quarterback, who is looking to throw the football.

HERE'S WHERE THE FIVE OFFENSIVE LINEMAN POSITIONS LINE UP ON THE FIELD. THE JOB OF THE OFFENSIVE LINE IS TO BLOCK DEFENDERS SO THEY CAN'T REACH THE FOOTBALL.

PROTECTING THE QUARTERBACK

LINE OF SCRIMMAGE

X   X   X   X   X

TACKLE   GUARD   CENTER   GUARD   TACKLE

X

QUARTERBACK

RUN THE BALL

Another important offensive position in football is the running back. This is the offensive player who runs the football. Before the snap, they line up behind or next to the quarterback. When they are given the football on a running play, it's called a handoff.

Most running backs are fast runners and have good hands. They have to see open space on the field made by blockers to run through. If they lose a football, it's called a fumble. Some running backs are big and bowl over blockers. Other running backs run past blockers or stop and start to make blockers miss tackles. They might also catch passes from the quarterback.

HALF OR FULL?

Running backs are sometimes called halfbacks, but another kind of running back is the fullback. They also stand behind the quarterback, but often don't run with the football. Instead, they block by running to meet defenders and blocking them. Some fullbacks catch passes, but many are only used to block further down the field.

TEAMS OFTEN HAVE A FEW GOOD RUNNING BACKS SO THEY CAN TAKE A BREAK IF THEY GET TIRED. BOSTON MILITIA RUNNING BACK WHITNEY ZELEE SHARES TIME WITH OTHER MILITIA RUNNING BACKS IN THE WOMEN'S FOOTBALL ALLIANCE.

OUT WIDE

The main target for a quarterback's throws is a wide receiver. This player stands out wide away from the offensive line and near the sidelines. Wide receivers, also called wideouts, run to certain places on the field to catch the ball thrown by the quarterback.

Where they run is decided by what play their team runs on offense. The pattern a wideout runs is called a route. Wide receivers work closely with quarterbacks to complete passes and move the ball down the field. Wide receivers have to be fast enough to beat defenders and have great hands to catch tough throws.

LOAD THEM UP

Most passing plays put at least one wide receiver on each side of the offensive line. But some plays put three wideouts on the same side. This is called a "trips" package. Sometimes all three run routes and can catch. Other times, two become blockers for the player that catches the ball!

WIDE RECEIVERS ALSO HAVE TO **IMPROVISE!** WHEN A QUARTERBACK THROWS ON THE RUN, A WIDE RECEIVER MUST OFTEN BREAK AWAY FROM THEIR ROUTE TO GET AWAY FROM THE DEFENSE AND BE OPEN TO CATCH A PASS.

END OF THE LINE

Another player that catches passes is called a tight end. These players are often called a hybrid, or mix, of a wide receiver and offensive lineman. Tight ends are often bigger and stronger than wideouts because they often start plays on the left or right side of an offensive line. There, they help block for running plays.

On passing plays, tight ends run routes just like wide receivers. Tight ends need to be good blockers and able to get away from bigger defenders if they want to catch passes. They need to be smart players because they're always in the middle of the action!

SWITCHING SPORTS

A good tight end is often tough for a defensive player to tackle. The size and strength of a strong blocker who also has good speed makes for a tough matchup in today's modern football game. Many great pro tight ends—like Antonio Gates and Rob Gronkowski—played basketball growing up. The skills they learned playing hoops help!

TIGHT ENDS CAN ALSO BE "SPLIT OUT" LIKE WIDE RECEIVERS ON PASSING PLAYS.

GET THE BALL

The job of the defense in football is simple: stop the other team from scoring. Defensive positions are all about matching up with what an offense is trying to do. That starts with the defensive line, which stands opposite the offensive line on the line of scrimmage.

The defensive line has two main positions: defensive end (DE) and defensive tackle (DT). Tackles play in the middle of the line, and DEs play at the end. The defensive line's job is to get past offensive blockers and tackle the ball carrier. They either get to the quarterback before they throw or tackle the player who has the ball.

3-4 OR 4-3?

There are two major types of defense in football. Their names come from the number of players a team puts on the defensive line. If a defense has two defensive ends and two defensive tackles, they run a 4-3 **scheme** because they have a 4-man defensive front and three linebackers. If they have three defensive linemen and four linebackers, they have a 3-4 defense.

IF THE DEFENSE TACKLES THE QUARTERBACK BEHIND THE LINE OF SCRIMMAGE, IT'S CALLED A SACK!

BACK THEM UP

Linebackers are the most **flexible** of the defensive positions. They "back" the defensive line and often play in groups of three or four. Linebackers are often faster and smaller than defensive linemen because they need to cover more ground on the field.

Depending on the play, a linebacker can rush the quarterback, cover a tight end, or track down a speedy running back. Linebackers need to be smart and **react** quickly to changing plays. An offense will try to get these players out of position in order to gain yards and score points.

SIDE TO SIDE

Linebackers have different positions just like the defensive linemen do. Outside linebackers (OLBs) start plays behind defensive ends. Inside linebackers, also called middle linebackers, play in the middle of the field. Linebackers are trouble for an offense because they can rush more players than the line can block!

LINEBACKERS OFTEN LEAD A TEAM IN TACKLES BECAUSE THEY MAKE PLAYS ALL OVER THE FIELD. THEY'RE VERY STRONG, BUT NEED TO BE FAST, TOO!

HEAD TO HEAD

A speedy wide receiver is a cornerback's worst nightmare. Cornerbacks face off against wideouts on every play. Their job is to stop the quarterback from throwing to a receiver for a lot of yards for a big gain. They need to be fast and have great **reflexes** to make fast, **athletic** plays on the football.

Cornerbacks get help from other players, but their goal is to "cover" a receiver so well that the quarterback can't throw the ball their way. If a pass does come, cornerbacks try to catch it. This is called an interception.

NO PENALTIES!

Cornerbacks have to be careful not to take **penalties** while defending wide receivers. A "pass interference" penalty can give the offense the ball at the spot where the penalty occurred. That can be a lot of free yards! Football has lots of rules that defenses have to follow so they don't give up touchdowns.

A TEAM'S BEST CORNERBACK OFTEN PLAYS AGAINST AN OPPONENT'S BEST WIDE RECEIVER. IT'S A TOUGH JOB!

SIT AND WAIT

The safety is the last line of defense in football. Safeties play far away from the line of scrimmage and wait for the play to come to them. Some safeties read a play and run back to the line of scrimmage to tackle a running back. Others race in to sack a quarterback!

Most safeties help out cornerbacks and linebackers covering players the quarterback may throw to. But pro football defenses have many moving parts, and a wide receiver may become a player the safety covers if the wideout runs to a certain place on the field. Sometimes these switches don't work, though. That's when a defense gives up a big play!

FREE OR STRONG?

Most schemes have two safeties on the field, sometimes called free and strong safeties. The strong safety plays opposite the offense's "strong" side, or the side where the tight end lines up. Strong safeties are often bigger than free safeties and worry about the run game, too. Free safeties, meanwhile, hang back and worry more about the passing game.

KICK IT

One of the most important positions in football is called a place kicker. They kick a football between the goal posts at the end of a football field. Their job is to make field goals—worth three points—and extra points after touchdowns are scored.

Field goal kickers need to be **accurate**—they have to put a football through small goal posts that are often very far away. It takes a lot of practice to learn how to kick a football the right way. If it's too low, the other team might block the kick!

PUNT IT

Punters are a different kind of kicker. They drop the ball on their foot as it's swinging to boot it a long way. Punters are used to kick the ball away if a team can't move the ball down the field fast enough. Bad offenses that can't get **first downs** use their punters a lot!

YOU MIGHT NOT THINK IT, BUT KICKERS SCORE A LOT OF POINTS. THINK OF ALL THE EXTRA POINTS THEY KICK AFTER TOUCHDOWNS. THEY OFTEN LEAD TEAMS IN SCORING EACH YEAR!

VERY SPECIAL

There are three main phases, or parts, of a football game—offense, defense, and special teams. Special teams plays are mostly kicks like a kickoff, which give the opponent the ball to start a game or after the other team scores.

Special teams players are often backups on offense and defense. But they still have very important jobs. Special teams **units** work together to make sure they know what each player needs to do on a play, whether it's blocking in a certain spot or returning a kick or punt a certain way. A mistake on special teams can cost a team a win!

TRICKS!

An onside kick happens on a kickoff when a team tries to recover the ball instead of kicking it away to the other team. After the ball goes 10 yards, the kicking team tries to recover it. Other teams try fake punts or field goals where they will try to run or throw for a first down instead of kicking the ball away!

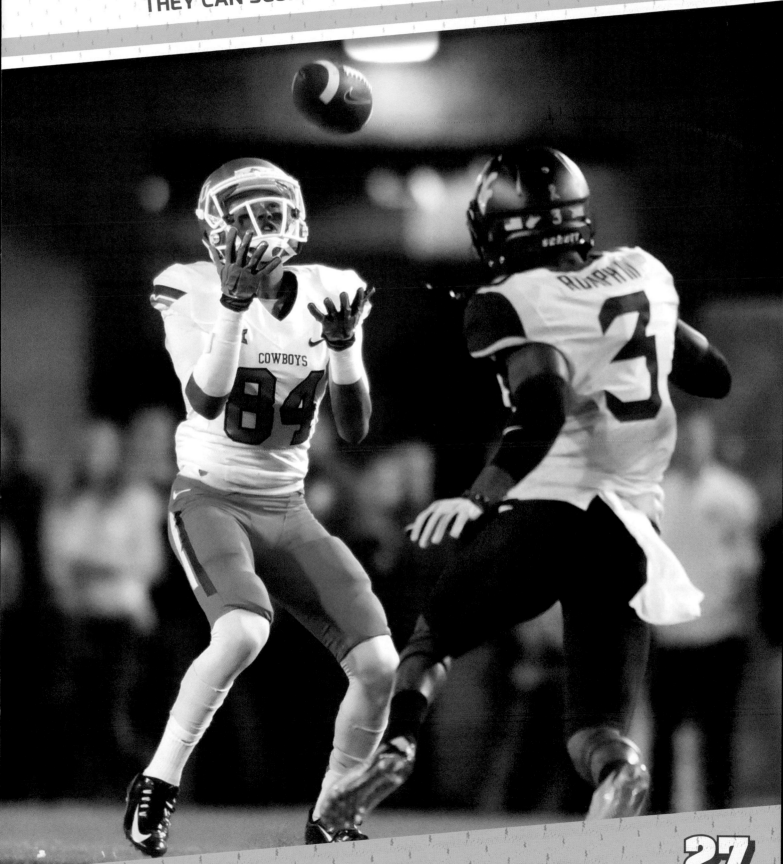

KICK AND PUNT RETURNERS ARE OFTEN THE FASTEST PLAYERS ON THE TEAM. THEY ARE VERY IMPORTANT IF THEY CAN SCORE TOUCHDOWNS ON KICK RETURNS!

KEEP PLAYING

Now that you have the basic positions in football down, let's dive into the playbook and have some fun. Did you know a running back or wide receiver can throw a pass like a quarterback? A player behind the line of scrimmage can throw a forward pass. They can even throw it to a quarterback!

Sometimes an offensive lineman can catch a pass! There are lots of rules and odd plays in football still left to learn. Keep watching football—and playing if you have the right safety equipment—to see what else you can learn about this fast-paced and fun game.

COACH 'EM UP

Some of the most important people in football aren't players, but coaches. They tell players what to do and how to play their positions. The head coach makes a lot of important decisions for a team, like when to run certain plays and what to do late in games. It's a tough job, but a good coach can help make a good team!

THERE'S A LOT YOU CAN LEARN FROM YOUR COACHES AND TEAMMATES. PAY ATTENTION AND HELP OUT OTHERS WHEN YOU CAN.

GLOSSARY

accurate: free from mistakes; able to hit the target

athletic: strong and able to play a sport a long time at a high level

equipment: the tools needed for a certain purpose

first down: gaining 10 yards in football on four or fewer plays

flexible: able to be used or shaped in a variety of ways

improvise: to make something happen without planning

opponent: a member of the other team in a game

penalty: loss or harm because of a broken rule

pocket: an area behind the line of scrimmage where quarterbacks are protected by the offensive line and can throw the football

react: to act in response

reflexes: the power to act quickly

scheme: a type of plan or lineup used to defend in football

snap: the start of a play in football where the center throws the ball backward between their legs to the quarterback

unit: a group working together

FOR MORE INFORMATION

BOOKS

Challen, Paul. *What Does a Quarterback Do?* New York, NY: PowerKids Press, 2015.

Hetrick, Hans. *Football's Record Breakers*. North Mankato, MN: Capstone Press, 2017.

Pelt, Don Van, and Brian Wingate. *An Insider's Guide to Football*. New York, NY: Rosen Central, 2015.

WEBSITES

All of the Football Positions, Explained
stack.com/a/football-positions
Find out what everyone on a football field does on this site.

Football: Player Positions
ducksters.com/sports/footballplayerpositions.php
Discover more player positions and how to play football here.

NFL Rule Book: How the Players Line Up
nfl.com/rulebook/lineup
Learn more about each position and what they do here.

INDEX